HIDDEN IN MY HEART

A TCK'S JOURNEY

THROUGH CULTURAL TRANSITION

TAYLOR MURRAY

BottomLine
► MEDIA

Hidden in My Heart:
A TCK's Journey Through Cultural Transition

by Taylor Murray

Copyright ©2013 Taylor Murray

Trade paperback ISBN: 978-0-9852192-5-3
Ebook ISBN: 978-0-9852192-6-0

Cover design by Vanessa Maynard
Cover and author photo by Sydney Murray

Hidden in My Heart is also available on Amazon
Kindle and Apple iBooks.

BottomLine Media, an imprint of Pioneers, publishes
materials that celebrate the "bottom line" of God's
covenant with Abraham: "I will bless all nations
through you." To purchase other BottomLine titles,
visit *Pioneers.org/Store*.

Pioneers is an international movement that mobilizes
teams to initiate church-planting movements among
unreached people groups. To get involved, visit
Pioneers.org.

DEDICATION

· · · · · · · · · · · ·

To Nana. Even during the worst days of your battle with cancer, you challenged me to always love, always forgive and always trust, even as I explored my deepest heart questions.

To my sister Sydney, who has shared all of these experiences with me, and to my newly-adopted sisters Alyssa, Morgan and Madison. I pray that these letters will encourage you as you begin your own TCK story.

PRAISE FOR HIDDEN IN MY HEART

What an amazing book! The writing and insights expressed demonstrate an intellectual and spiritual maturity well past the author's fourteen years of age. I commend her as I was 39 before I began to understand how my life, like hers, had been impacted by having grown up among many cultural worlds. Taylor's writing speaks to all who have known the paradox of living in this world of rich experience, yet felt the pain of never fully belonging to one place or the other. Her insights, her awareness of the process that is going on within her, will help all who are currently living in this way understand their own story. In addition, it will give clearer vision for those who also grew up in the neither/nor world of a cross-cultural childhood and never had language for their experiences. *Hidden in My Heart* is a great new addition to helping many others have clearer vision for what they or others they love are going through.

Ruth E. Van Reken
crossculturalkid.org
author of *Third Culture Kids: Growing Up Among Worlds*
and *Letters Never Sent*

A Third Culture Kid (TCK) is a person who has spent a significant part of his or her developmental years outside the parents' culture. The TCK frequently builds relationships to all of the cultures, while not having full ownership in any. Although elements from each culture may be assimilated into the TCK's life experience, the sense of belonging is in relationship to others of similar background.

from *Third Culture Kids: Growing Up Among Worlds*
by David C. Pollock and Ruth E. Van Reken

A NOTE TO PARENTS

Transitioning to a different culture is challenging for parents and their children. We were in our mid-forties, trying to learn a new language, serving in Japanese churches, homeschooling our twin daughters and basically just trying to survive. I remember the pressure that I felt as a mother to help our family transition smoothly. I felt like everyone's heart was in my hand, and I was supposed to make everyone emotionally happy. I was overwhelmed. It wasn't until later that God showed me that all of our hearts are in His hand.

As we watched Taylor, we thought she was handling things the best of all of us. She always smiled. During our first two terms in Japan, we talked with her frequently about the transition. In the midst of it all, she truly couldn't discern how she was feeling, and we didn't know the right questions to ask. None of us knew what was "hidden in her heart."

On our first home assignment, Taylor realized that she no longer fit in the American "teen" scene, and she knew she didn't fit in our Japanese world. Upon returning to Japan, she tried even harder to fit. She wanted to be a "good missionary kid." But the language and cultural challenges overcame her. She withdrew. Even though our family relationships deepened and her best friends became those other TCKs that she met each year at conference, she still could not understand the aching and gnawing of her heart. She was growing spiritually, but God wanted to teach her deeper lessons of faith and trust.

At the time of this writing, my mother is dying from bone cancer. We have been in America for a year because I am her caregiver. During this quiet year in my mom's townhome, God has worked mightily in our hearts. my mom said, "Go back. God has work for you to do in Japan." We stayed, knowing that God had work to do in our lives as we cared for her. After a few months in America, we were shocked when we experienced Taylor's subtle anger. We knew we had to help her understand what she was feeling and why, so we took this journey with her. We pushed her to go deeper and to take her emotions to God. What a learning experience it has been for all of us. God is writing His story in each of our lives.

As we read her letters to God, we were surprised how she had perceived the events and how these events were shaping her. We cried. We had no idea what was occurring in her little heart and no idea of the bitter root that was sprouting and beginning to bear fruit. We praise God that He intervened by providing the time and circumstances for her to reflect. When she wrote these letters to God, she wrote only to Him. These letters are her raw emotions and honest questions. Later we thought the letters might help other TCKs who are experiencing similar emotions and the resulting shame or confusion.

We are now preparing to return to the field with three young, newly-adopted daughters, in addition to our older twins. Because God has allowed us to better understand the unique journey of one of our TCK daughters, we feel more prepared to ask the right questions and guard the experiences of our other girls. May God bless you and guide you as you nurture and guide your own TCK.

Scott & Susan Murray

PERSONAL NOTE TO READERS

This book is about my struggles as a TCK. It's about my fear of the unknown, my fear of taking risks and my fear of letting others inside my heart. My emotions while transitioning into a new culture may be different from other TCKs, but I believe we all hide fear, grief and anger in our hearts... maybe just in different ways than I have.

These prayers are so very personal. I've questioned God's goodness, and I've realized how fearful I actually was. I've uncovered my self-centered nature, and I've revealed stories that I would rather keep hidden. I felt so unworthy of God's forgiveness as I wrote these prayers, but I realize now, it just shows how desperately I need His grace.

Japan is truly my home now. I realize, though, that I will never really fit in. I will never be fully bilingual. I will never truly understand their culture. But that's not what God's called me to strive for. He's called me to strive to be like Him. He placed me in hard situations, but I was the one who chose how to deal with them. I changed my goal from striving after Him to striving to be like the Japanese people. The emotions I experienced during those difficult situations were mine. They weren't created by the people, the culture or the language. Instead, they originated from my own anger and fear—my own desire to belong and my own selfishness in wanting to be truly accepted.

This is my TCK story. These are my prayers to God. This is what I discovered when I searched for answers... answers that could only be found by acknowledging the emotions hidden in my heart.

CONTENTS

• • • • • • • •

CHAPTER ONE
· · · · · · · · · · · ·

Introduction

I never knew a TCK's life could be so challenging. So painful. So humbling. So stretching. But then again, I never knew what a TCK was until I became one.

When we first moved to Japan, I was just 9 years old. I plowed through the first couple months, reminding myself that this was an adventure, an adventure that God had called my family to take. I wouldn't allow doubts and questions to enter my mind, and if they ever did creep up unexpectedly, I would shove them down in my heart, reminding myself firmly to not bring them up again.

After six months, I couldn't shove my frustration and questions down any further, and they began bubbling much too close to the surface of my heart. That's when panic struck and reality hit. That's when I realized that this was our home for years to come, and I wasn't calling it an adventure anymore. Though amazing, the culture was difficult to understand, and the language barred me in a way that I had never expected.

By shoving my feelings of anger and bitterness deeper into my heart, I was making it much worse. Instead of dealing with my emotions one by one, I was letting them grow to a point where I couldn't stuff them down any more... and they were becoming a flame. I was angry!

I realize now that my anger was unresolved grief. I had left everything that I knew—the States, my home, my extended family—for everything I didn't know. My sorrow turned into anger, an anger that had to be directed toward someone. As I looked around at my life, I asked myself, *Who had taken away everything? Who was making my life challenging?* My answer was God, and I quickly directed my anger toward Him.

> *I had left everything I knew—the States, my home, my extended family—for everything I didn't know.*

I am now 14, and we are on home assignment (furlough). God has asked me to open up my heart and finally process the emotions that I have shoved deep into my heart. As I've allowed my doubts and questions to surface, I've discovered my anger toward God and have recognized my emptiness and sorrow over past losses.

I began this journey by writing a list of emotions that I felt over the past four years, and I began writing letters to God about each emotion. I wrote my perspective and then thought through what God's perspective might have been. It's been amazing what I have discovered during this time with God.

Through these prayers, He revealed to me His part of this story: His brokenness over my brokenness and His hurt over mine. He's lovingly taught me the lessons He was trying to teach me and has given me the strength He was so readily offering. Through this time of learning, I have felt God's amazing presence. He asked me to take a step of faith, to trust in

Him as I forgive and ask forgiveness, and to hold His hand as He guides me through an amazing journey of truth.

In this book, I have written to God what I had wished I had written in the midst of both the hardships and joy, and I have relived the emotions that I wished I had understood while I was experiencing them. What I have written has come directly from my heart. Somehow, I feel that God is truly the Author of this book, not me. Though humbling, my understanding of God and His love for me has grown so much bigger, and my relationship with Him has grown that much closer. I haven't necessarily written this book for God. I feel like He has written this book through me. I find it so overwhelming when I take a step back and realize how God displayed my well-hidden ugliness and then used it to ultimately glorify Him.

CHAPTER TWO
· · · · · · · · · · · · ·

I Feel Like a Failure in This Culture

Dear God, "You haven't learned much Japanese, have you? It's been four years, and I assumed you would have picked it up quicker than you have." I could hear the question in my teacher's voice, along with a hint of reprimand coupled with disappointment.

We had begun to visit an older couple's house for language study each Friday evening for about a year now. We were starting to build closer relationships with them. Slowly but surely I was letting You help me overcome my fear of language. You were giving me courage to leave my comfort zone for the first time in over three years. I was so excited that evening during language class. The desire to speak completely in Japanese encouraged me to try my hardest that particular evening... until now.

I tried to ignore the remark as he repeated it again to my sister, Sydney, because she hadn't understood what he'd said. Lifting my drink to my lips, the steaming tea burned my mouth as I swallowed it quickly. I considered the options of my reply. If I nodded, wouldn't that seem like I agreed with him? And if I shook my head, that would be arrogant—and so untrue. I took another sip of my tea and didn't make eye contact. Playing with my pencil, I hoped he would assume I thought his question was rhetorical, though I knew just as well as he did that it wasn't.

We had just finished our "one-minute speeches"—a time when we would pick an experience during our week and try to explain it to him in Japanese. My "one-minute speech" was filled with pauses and "ums," but I was happy when I had finished it with little help from my teacher. I had hoped I would meet his expectations that evening, but from his comment, I hadn't. I tried to force myself to let his critique go, but it had hurt me more than I cared to admit. I wondered why it had to be the evening when I was so determined to step out of my comfort zone that he decided to tell me that my Japanese was lacking.

> *I tried to force myself to let his critique go, but it had hurt me more than I cared to admit.*

I didn't question the reprimand and certainly not the implications. I, too, thought Japanese would be much easier than it turned out to be, but the disappointment in his voice was what hurt me the most. I value how people perceive me, how I look in their eyes. When he acknowledged his disappointment, I felt as though I had failed him somehow. I hated to be the source of disappointment and pain, and it hurt me when I realized that I hadn't measured up to his expectations.

I wasn't angry at first, but as time went on, and our lesson was finished, anger began to bring my feelings of failure to the surface. I could feel Satan winning the battle inside me. God, You wanted me to forgive, while Satan was asking me why I should. You were reminding me that my teacher hadn't intentionally hurt my feelings. Instead, he had practiced the Japanese way of encouraging someone younger than himself to keep learning. Satan was surfacing past feelings of failure. It was so much easier to believe the lies Satan had placed in front of me.

In the midst of my anger and hurt, forgiveness just seemed too hard. I know my teacher didn't mean to hurt my feelings; he was just trying to encourage me. Even though he doesn't realize his hurtful words, I want to forgive him, God. But it is so hard to forgive when I keep hearing the same words of "failure." Can you help me...?

Love,
Taylor

WHAT'S HIDDEN IN YOUR HEART?

- In your cultural context, what are the areas where you feel like a failure?

- How would you define "failure"?

- Can you think of a story when a national unintentionally pointed out how you "fail" in this culture?

- How does bitterness of the heart impact your love for people?

- When you repeatedly feel like a failure, what do you do? How do you handle all the negative emotions?

- If your current situation is God's "best" for you, then how do you accept the challenges of not being able to succeed?

CHAPTER THREE

· · · · · · · · · · · · · ·

I Feel So Much Resentment Toward the People I'm Supposed to Love

Dear God, I was so frustrated. Clenching my fists, I looked down, trying to hide beneath my thick winter coat. Did the people around me actually realize how blatant their stares were? The lady beside me hadn't looked down yet, and I could feel my anger building. Expression curious and eyes wide, she groped for her shopping cart, refusing to look away. I gritted my teeth and walked in the opposite direction, face burning. It was so humiliating to be stared at. Their openness in staring made me feel so much like the foreigner.

We went to the mall many times. I remember going there a few months after moving. We were still such a novelty, and stares were frequent and obvious. I had tried to prepare myself for them, but I was taken completely by surprise.

It was exciting at first...being treated like someone special. Japanese people would stare at my blonde hair and blue eyes in amazement. But after a few months of continual, open stares, the excitement began to fade quickly. I wanted to fit in, to be treated like a normal Japanese person. I wanted to have a true friend. I wanted to live like everyone else.

But the stares, it seemed, would never stop. The blatancy of some unnerved me, and resentment quickly started to build in my heart. I felt like an attraction, not a spiritual light in the midst of darkness! Before moving to Japan, people had reminded me to shine brightly. Instead, I felt like a nail sticking out crookedly amidst lines of perfectly even, identical nails.

Right then, I was just too angry to realize my advantage. It never crossed my mind that the attention I was receiving because of my nationality gave me the perfect opportunity to shine brightly. I was taking the attention negatively, not taking advantage of it. When I caught people's stares, my smiles quickly turned into frowns of annoyance. And though I didn't realize it, my resentment began to construct a strong and steady wall of anger.

I wanted to fit in, to be treated like a normal Japanese person. I wanted to have a true friend.

I was so frustrated with You, God. I realized my resentfulness and knew it was wrong. I was confused why You hadn't chosen someone else to go to Japan—someone who could deal with the attention in a better way. Why hadn't you chosen someone whose smiles grew bigger as stares grew more blatant? More hearts would be won and stronger relationships would have been built. I sensed my weakness and hated my annoyance, but I couldn't change my feelings. I couldn't reverse my attitude. I was a foreigner in a foreign country. Did I expect that I would fit in?

I realize now what You were trying to do. When the walls of my resentment finally tumbled to the ground and my heart was torn and bruised, I had a decision to make. I could choose to allow you to shine through my weakness, letting your strength and power penetrate through the heavy destruction littering my heart, or I could choose to gather the broken pieces and begin to construct yet another shaky building of anger and resentment.

You were beside me the whole time, God. You were urging me to make the first choice, the right choice. You knew that a wall of anger and resentment could only be built so far before it would become shaky and weak. When it fell, You knew it would leave me with questions, searching for strength. That's why You were beside me the whole time I was resenting You for the wall I was creating.

You were counteracting my anger with Your love, reminding me where true strength comes from and urging me to trust You. I want to trust You now, God, and depend on Your unseen strength so that Your power will shine through my sin and weakness. I realize now that *that* would be the greatest testimony of all. I'm not sure how, though. Can you teach me how to use the attention for Your glory?

Love,
Taylor

WHAT'S HIDDEN IN YOUR HEART?

- Do you "stand out" in your cultural context? What makes you different?

- How do you handle the stares when people see the physical difference or the language challenges?

- Can you think of a situation when you had no compassion for the people where you are trying to share the Good News?

- What are some concrete ways to use the attention for a spiritual advantage to glorify God?

CHAPTER FOUR
· · · · · · · · · · · · · ·

I Feel Discontent Because My
American Body Is So Different

Dear God, pushing the heavy gate of the preschool open, I shifted my bag to my other shoulder and walked to the shoe shelves. Slipping off my shoes, which is a normal Japanese custom, I slid them into an open shelf. My hands shook as I put on my indoor shoes. I took a deep breath before sliding open the glass door to the office. It was mandatory to ask for permission to go to the gymnastics room, a large area above a local preschool which was used for gymnastics lessons. I had to learn to say it in Japanese weeks earlier. *And I was nervous.*

Before starting gymnastics, we had practiced the introduction for weeks. I even had a copy of it in my bag just in case. At the moment, I wished we had never signed up for gymnastics. I never imagined the challenges and discontentment I would feel, and I didn't realize how many things You would ask me to accept and lay down during that year.

From the very beginning, I realized how inflexible I was. My twin sister, Sydney, and I were both so different from the other Japanese girls. They understood what the teacher was saying, had been taking gymnastics since preschool and were very flexible. Sydney and I had never participated in a sport like this one before. We weren't very flexible, and we didn't understand what the teacher was trying to tell us.

I finished my introduction quickly, thankful that I hadn't needed my paper. It was embarrassing when I had to use it in front of the teachers. Hurrying up the steps, I opened the door to the gymnastics room and bowed to my teacher. Placing my bag on the mats in the back, I took my place next to a few Japanese girls my age. Bringing my legs up to my chest, I laced my fingers around my legs. I didn't know the position we were supposed to sit in the first time we went to gymnastics, and the teacher's wife had to tell us that we couldn't sit on our knees.

I looked around that afternoon, once again noticing the difference between our bodies and theirs. They were tiny and could bend in lots of ways, where I was tall and big-boned next to the other Japanese girls my age. Over the next couple of months, I grew very discontent with my body. I hated the way I felt next to the other girls, and I hated my ignorance and clumsiness. Most Wednesday afternoons, I just wanted to crawl into a hole, and tonight was another prime example.

After the beginning exercises, the teacher told everyone that we were going to do flips on the bars. It was my first time doing flips, and I was excited to learn something new. We stood in a line as the teacher prepared the bars. His wife tried to explain to us what we were supposed to do, but I was confused and decided to watch the other girls before me. As it grew closer to my turn, I started to get nervous. The girls ran to the bar and held it as they flipped over. Our teacher would help them flip over the bar and land on their feet. It looked easy enough.

When it was my turn, I ran up to the bar and grabbed it. My teacher tried to help me flip over the bar, but when I glanced up at him, heat flooded my face. He was having a hard time lifting me up. "You're heavy, aren't you?" he asked me a few minutes later. I didn't know how to respond to the question. *Was I that heavy?*

I tried to help him, finishing the flip as quickly as I could. I could see the Japanese children grinning as I walked to the back of the line. Fighting tears, I balled my fists. I looked down at my own body, and then at the other Japanese girls' bodies. *Yuck.*

The Bible says that You created me the way You want me to be, and I wondered if You had purposefully made me tall and big so that I wouldn't fit in. You said that I was beautiful and perfect in Your sight, but right then, I felt ugly and out of place.

You had created me exactly how You wanted, and who was I to question Your purpose in doing so?

But, God, it wasn't my responsibility to worry about whether I fit in or not, whether I was flexible or tiny, whether I could understand the teacher or not. I realize now that You had called me to serve—to serve and to shine. Maybe I was tall, and maybe I was big compared to the other Japanese girls my age, but did it really matter? No. It didn't.

You had created me exactly how You wanted, and who was I to question Your purpose in doing so? It was so much easier to accept discontentment than to know the truth about myself. Japan had humbled me in so many areas, and pride was something I clung to like life itself. Asking me to lay down my pride was like asking me to surrender my body fully to You, and I already had felt like You had failed me in so many areas. I wanted to keep something to myself.

But God, I realize now, You weren't the one failing me! I was the one ignoring You! You were begging me to surrender my discontentment and pride, to give the heavy burden that I carried to You. But I refused. Now I see that though Your request was much harder, in the end it would have brought so much inner peace. If I would have accepted my body and laid down my pride, You would have begun to mold me into something beautiful, something shining for Your glory, not for others.

Now I see that's all that really matters. God, I still struggle with my body, but I want to lay it down and surrender fully to You. I want to lay down my pride and give You my everything, so that You can mold me into someone closer to You.

Love,
Taylor

WHAT'S HIDDEN IN YOUR HEART?

· What are some of your physical qualities that you resent or would like to change?

· If someone is discontent with their body or intellect, what things might they say or do?

· How has your cultural context contributed to your opinion of yourself?

· God says we were created wonderfully, but how do we actually believe it when we see something else?

· How do we trust God that His plan for us is good?

CHAPTER FIVE

· · · · · · · · · · · ·

I Feel Discouraged Because of My Cluelessness

Dear God, wiping my sweaty hands on my dress, I exhaled quickly as I turned from the woman at the desk. Head bent, she added my name to a list of students and told me to wait until the heavy wooden doors opened for orientation. Before turning, I had glanced down at my name on the clipboard lying on the desk behind me. My name was the only one written in Katakana (the alphabet for foreign names). The rest were written in Kanji (the characters for Japanese names).

This was the first time that I would play at a piano recital. I had practiced diligently and wanted it to be perfect. As I looked down at the sheet before me, I could feel Satan's lies and began to hear his convincing whispers.

Heart dropping, I bowed my head as I waited to be called into orientation. I knew that I was the foreigner—but did they have to use a completely different alphabet to differentiate it? I didn't like that feeling—that knot in my stomach—when it hit me for the hundredth time that I'm not the same as everybody else. I am the stranger.

As I think about it now, I was frustrated that everyone stared at me. But if our places were reversed, wouldn't I be doing the same thing? I was a blonde-haired, blue-eyed foreigner wanting to perform in a Japanese piano recital! They didn't know me or even know I was taking piano lessons at Yamaha School of Music. When my name was called, I waved goodbye to my family and followed the other Japanese students into the large room where we would be performing. The teachers explained what we were supposed to do and when we were supposed to leave the room to follow a teacher backstage. I tried hard to listen carefully, but I didn't understand most of it.

I was frustrated that everyone stared at me. But if our places were reversed, wouldn't I be doing the same thing?

After my teacher finished briefing the other kids, she called me over. I squeezed past the 25 Japanese children sitting next to me, feeling all 25 eyes focused on me as I followed the teacher to the back of the room. Discouragement threatened to overwhelm me as I read the English instructions one of the Yamaha teachers had written for me.

Though the instructions were well intended, I hated the fact that I couldn't understand what the other, normal kids understood. I realized, once again, that I was another problem. As I looked down at the translation, I realized all the work put into writing it. They wouldn't have to do this if I weren't there. I could feel my tears already gather as I returned to my seat. How could I be so clueless?

A battle seemed to rage inside of me as the parents slowly filed in. I felt like Satan reminded me again and again that my cluelessness created hardships for everyone. I became so discouraged that I thought I should quit. Why bother? Even when I try, I don't know what is happening. I began to drown in discouragement. The piano recital was over before I knew it, and I never wanted to do it again. So, God, how can You be my encouragement in situations like this? How can I keep placing myself in circumstances where my cluelessness overwhelms me and everyone else? How do I depend upon You?

Love,
Taylor

WHAT'S HIDDEN IN YOUR HEART?

- Can you think of a time when you were overwhelmed by your own cluelessness?

- When discouragement settles into your heart, what do you do?

- How can God's Word encourage us?

CHAPTER SIX

I Feel Bitter Because of All the Expectations

Dear God, summoning my courage, I glanced down at the song sheet in my hand, skimming over the Japanese Sunday school song one more time. I knew the song by heart. The three months of practice with my family after dinner had ensured that I would remember the song for months to come. Flipping the sheet over, I glanced through the Ten Commandments one more time. The teachers were calling us to practice before we would sing in the main service that Sunday, and I wanted to show them how much I had practiced. I wanted to show them that I was competent.

I dreaded the songs we had to sing and verses we had to memorize for our Sunday school class. While it took the Japanese kids a few weeks to memorize the songs and verses for the service, we were given the verse and songs months in advance. My sister and I would practice and practice until we knew the songs by heart.

While we were practicing before the main service, we were all nervous. I knew that, but this was only my second time singing in church. The other children knew the song and verse perfectly, and they sang it quickly with ease. I started off okay, but when I made a mistake I couldn't get back on track. That is when panic hit. What if all the preparation and work was in vain? What if I couldn't do it? *God... help me... what do I do?* I stood next to the children, head ducked as they finished the song. I was so ashamed and frustrated. *I can't do anything, can I? Is this how it will be?*

I had worked for months on this song, and to everyone else, it appeared as though I hadn't even reviewed it before church that day. The teachers came up to me after we had finished singing the song, disappointment framing their faces. "Did you practice the song? We gave it to you three months ago. We thought you would know it by now." I tried to explain to them that the pace was too fast, that I had practiced but I couldn't keep up. They didn't understand, and I didn't have the language to explain.

> *I was frustrated by the high expectations in Japan. I tried so hard to measure up ... and I couldn't.*

I left Sunday school in tears of bitterness and shame. I was incompetent to accomplish the smallest of challenges. Angry at You for not intervening, I wondered what I didn't understand. Why were You letting me go through all of this?

I heard Your voice pleading with me, "Come, Taylor, take my hand. I love you so much, but only I can see the bigger picture." I refused your pleadings, asking myself why I would yield to Your wishes when You had yet to answer mine in the way I wanted.

I was frustrated by the high expectations in Japan. I tried so hard to measure up, and I couldn't. Discouragement was blinding me from seeing my mistake: I was too focused on the wrong expectations. You weren't asking me to measure up in the Japanese eyes. You were only asking me to accomplish Your expectations. You didn't even care if I wasn't strong enough to do it on my own because You were offering to help me all along! You had called me to shine, to shine for You, to be a testimony of Your love, no matter the cost.

I want to accept Your strength now, God. I realize that I was only meant to see a small piece in the puzzle of Your plan. I want to rest in what I know and trust that You are strong enough to handle the details of my life.

Love,
Taylor

WHAT'S HIDDEN IN YOUR HEART?

- Can you think of a time when you prepared thoroughly and yet did not meet the expectations?

- Can you think of a time that was excruciatingly painful and you became angry at God because He did not intervene to help you?

- Can you think of a current song that connects to God's goodness during our hardships?

- How can we say that God is good yet sometimes it appears that He is not helping us?

- When you think about trying to "measure up" to all the expectations, where do these expectations come from?

- What are God's expectations for us?

CHAPTER SEVEN

I Feel Hopeless Because Language Hinders Every Situation

Dear God, hopelessness. I hate that feeling. The drop in your stomach when you realize what you want is just too far out of your reach. I feel that way about the Japanese language sometimes, and one Sunday at youth group was another prime example of the loss of hope and expectation.

A Christian university professor preached that morning, and his sermons always made me extra nervous. He always had complicated Japanese word games after the lessons, and we were expected to participate. I sat down in my seat and put my purse on the floor next to my chair. Feigning a look of excitement, I tried my hardest to hide my nerves. As the professor walked to the front of the room, I focused my attention on my hands. I couldn't understand a word he said. I knew that, but did he know that?

The staff tried hard to do what they could for us, and I never ever blamed them for not trying, but they could only do so much when it came to language. They couldn't speak English, and I couldn't speak Japanese. After the sermon and sharing time, we began the word game. The foreigners were placed throughout four or five different groups, and the leaders always cast a wary eye on their unusual participants.

Hopelessness had already begun to take control as I was passed two sheets of paper filled with Japanese. My mind had slowed as I skimmed over the Japanese, skipping kanji. It was useless. I couldn't understand any of it. The leader of our group tried to explain it to me, but I couldn't understand the Japanese. When it was my turn, I couldn't understand the questions to answer, and I didn't understand the answers to guess. The hopeless expression of the group leader staring back at me seemed to perfectly mirror my own.

How I longed to be Japanese! How I wished I was normal.

After a moment's hesitation, my group skipped me and moved on to the next person. Part of me felt lifted by relief, while the other part began to sink in anger and hopelessness. How I longed to be Japanese! How I wished I was normal. The Japanese were trying so hard to help me fit in, and I felt like their efforts were in vain. I felt so much like a problem. I couldn't shake the feeling of utter failure. This had happened again and again. I wondered if I would ever be able to play a Japanese word game. At that moment when hopelessness seemed to be crushing me, I highly doubted it.

At that point, I wasn't angry at You. I was confused, but too defeated to ask why. Hopelessness had drained any determination left, leaving a mind too tired to try on my next turn. This was yet another situation where language had barred me from participating, and I was tired of it.

I understand now what You were trying to teach me. You had

moved me to a different country where speaking hindered everything. You were asking me to fully accept what You had given me, find the joy in each situation, and rest in it. Instead, I was allowing myself to be paralyzed by fear... and blamed others for it. God, I want to accept the circumstances that You have placed me in and rest in the peace that You so readily provide.

Yet this is all so easy to say. We will return to Japan soon. What will I do when I am placed in the exact same situation? Even though I have been studying for four years, I am not fluent. The language still bars me from belonging and participating. How can I not be discouraged when it feels hopeless?

Love,
Taylor

Dear God, I glanced up at the college student next to me as she translated the sermon point into Japanese-English, which is sometimes difficult to understand. I was so thankful that she was translating the main points of the sermon. Though it was only about four points, the 45-minute sermon seemed that much longer when I didn't understand anything at all.

After the sermon was finished, we were divided into small groups for sharing time. I was confident that our leader wouldn't ask us to share what we learned because they knew we hadn't understood the lesson. I was placed into a group with a boy and a few girls. We started with the leader and went around in a circle, sharing what we learned from the sermon.

"It's your turn now, Taylor." I looked up in surprise. "Can you share what you learned?" My heart flipped.

"I'm sorry, I didn't understand what the lesson was about." I clenched my fists, heart skipping a beat at the next comment, "I saw a leader translate for you, though." *What was I sup-*

posed to say? It was only four lines in broken English. "Umm..."
*I couldn't say I didn't understand. That would sound awful and
would embarrass the leader who translated.*

"Did you not understand your leader?" she asked.

"Oh yes, I did! But she only translated a few lines." I quickly
replied, hoping she would understand.

"Oh." An awkward silence followed. I wanted to say something, but didn't know what. Why did language make everything so difficult?

> *Lord, you were there all along! You hadn't given me more than I could handle.*

I was frustrated. I
thought the leader
was being insensitive.
But how would she
have known, God?
Why did I blame it on
her? Most of the youth
group members have never been to different countries where
language is a huge barrier. They haven't experienced the confusion of trying to understand a different language. I was frustrated at them for their inexperience, and I was frustrated at You
for Your seeming lack of concern at what I could handle.

Because of the language barrier, awkward moments and
confusing activities, I've believed Satan's lie that You are
good to others, just not me! I believed that You were being
hard on me because You didn't care about my feelings. That
You were giving me too much and that I couldn't handle it all.
But, Lord, You were right there all along! You hadn't given me
more than I could handle because You were willingly offering
to help with what You had given to me.

You wanted me to unload my frustration and find peace in
You. I was thinking of all the things You had allowed me to go
through, and it was overwhelming me. You were wooing me to

give my frustration to You. God, I know that You are good to others. Help me trust that You are good to me. Help me trust that when You allow hard situations because of language, You want to use them to strengthen me and to glorify You.

Love,
Taylor

WHAT'S HIDDEN IN YOUR HEART?

- As a TCK, think about your language learning experience. How did lack of language bar you from "belonging"?

- Did you ever think you would never learn the language? What did you do with the feelings of hopelessness?

- When you learned the language, how did things change?

- How does God's Word give hope to the hopeless?

- What are the evidences in your life that God is good, not only to others but to you personally?

- Can you think of a time when you experienced a hardship but later saw God's plan to use the hardship to strengthen you and glorify Him?

CHAPTER EIGHT
· · · · · · · · · · · · ·

I Feel Embarrassed Because I Don't Understand
Japanese Culture

Dear God, it was my first time going to youth group camp. I wasn't exactly *dreading* it, but I was nervous and didn't know what to expect as a camper. I was so different than everyone else, and I was fearful that I would do something embarrassing because I didn't understand their unwritten cultural rules.

Before I went, I remember praying with my parents. I had begged You to be with me, to help me. And I was certain this would be a camp that I would remember—the camp where I truly connected with other Japanese girls.

It was a difficult ferry ride up to the camp. Everyone was more quiet than usual. This was the first time they had had a foreigner attend camp, and I could tell all of the staff were nervous.

The first day was sports day. The girls had to change in the gym while the boys went to the restrooms. I had packed a pair of sweat pants, a t-shirt, and socks. I had also cleaned my outdoor tennis shoes—trying to fit the cultural requirements. They weren't perfectly spotless, but I had told myself that they would do. It was a bit awkward changing in front of everyone else, and I was thankful when I was fully dressed for sports. But when I looked around, I saw that everyone else was dressed differently. They had specific indoor shoes, leggings under their gym shorts and sport jackets tied around their waists. I had cleaned my only pair of tennis shoes and wore sweat pants and a t-shirt. I packed for the traditional American sporting activity, and they packed for the Japanese!

I gritted my teeth and joined them, forcing myself not to think about how different I looked. When everyone gathered, they began sitting in rows according to their names that the Japanese leader was calling out. I couldn't understand why they were even sitting in rows! I listened for my name and quickly sat where the other kids on my team were sitting. As we were divided into groups, I heard some of the boys talking about my sister and I. "See?" they said. "They can't understand anything!"

I wanted to understand their ways so I observed everything. When everyone was in perfect lines, all sitting the same way, another staff member called out something else. Everyone stood. Confused, I stood a bit late. A man walked through the double doors. Everyone shouted something and bowed low. I was completely lost. What was everyone doing? Embarrassment had begun to build as I fumbled with a late bow and sat quickly.

The man took the next 20 minutes explaining the rules and showing us where the buildings were located in the camp. Though he used pictures, he was talking in a polite level of speech, and I couldn't understand anything he said. When the games finally started, I wanted to scream. I prayed that I wouldn't do something humiliating, but I somehow knew that *that* particular prayer was prayed in vain. Embarrassment was becoming a part of my life, it seemed, and as many times as I prayed for its departure, it always seemed to find a way to show its control in times such as these.

As the game started I asked You why you hadn't listened to my prayers, and I mocked myself for thinking that there was a chance I might understand the cultural clues. This was the first time I had played the game, and whenever I tried to play, I always messed up and allowed the other team to score more points. I could tell the kids on my team were trying to be patient with me, but they were starting to get annoyed.

By now, I was angry and embarrassed, trying to hold my tears until the last game ended. I was asking You why You always made my life so embarrassing. I hated the looks of annoyance on the other kids' faces, and I was angry and hurt. Why did You always do this to me?

I was so focused on my anger that I never stopped to think that my anger was actually directed toward You.

I was so focused on my anger that I never stopped to think that my anger was actually directed toward You. I never stopped to think of the pain in Your eyes as You looked down at me from above. At the way Your heart broke for me as you watched my struggle. At how much it hurt when I asked You why. As the day progressed and my embarrassment grew, I had questioned Your love, but I never questioned Your presence.

You were always right beside me, waiting for me to acknowledge You. I was blinded by my anger, and I refused to consider the possibility that You were trying to love me. If I hadn't been so focused on remaining in my comfort zone, You would have shown me Your strength and surrounded me with love.

I realize that I will never completely understand the Japanese culture. I will probably always fumble and do things a little differently. During these past four years of trying to learn the culture and messing up drastically, I allowed myself to turn my frustration into anger at You because You could have made it easier for me. But You didn't. I didn't give myself time to learn, time to understand. I expected to just "observe and know." I wasn't able to laugh at my mistakes. I am not Japanese, and I do not understand their culture. But You have called my family to serve there. You want me to accept the challenges, not to be embarrassed because I don't understand culture but to embrace the opportunity of learning something new.

Love,
Taylor

WHAT'S HIDDEN IN YOUR HEART?

· Can you list all of the cultural surprises that you have encountered as a TCK?

· Think of a time when you did something totally different than everyone else because you didn't know their "unwritten rules."

· What has been your most embarrassing culture mess-up?

· When cultural blunders occur, how can you approach it in a way to make yourself and others more comfortable?

· What are the best ways to learn and understand your new cultural context?

· How can you rely on God to help you through the cultural struggles?

CHAPTER NINE

. . . .

I Feel Anger Because of Careless Remarks

Dear God, heart hammering in my chest, I slipped into the pool's chilly water. Shivering, I ducked my head under the water and came up once more, exhaling slowly. Nerves jittery, I watched my teacher walk over. I had passed my breast stroke test the week before, and now we were to begin learning butterfly... the hardest stroke out of the four. I glanced at the boy next to me as he dipped under the lane divider into the other lane. He had the option of swimming in our lane or the next lane of difficulty. I half hoped he would choose our lane. But who would choose to swim with foreigners?

Swimming was always something that I never really looked forward to. My other swim mates were never very accepting, and the teachers, though kind, were blatantly curious. It made me feel uncomfortable and out of place. Our teacher came up and jumped into the pool. He caught my eye, smiling briefly before telling the Japanese boy that he needed to swim in our lane for that lesson. Since this was our first lesson learning butterfly, he needed some-one who was more advanced in that area to be an example.

Groaning, the boy quickly began begging to swim in the other lane. As the teacher explained the reason, his questions and pleas became more desperate. Glancing at us disappointingly, he tried once more to get out of swimming with us, but the teacher was adamant.

Was I that difficult to swim with? Was I so different that no one wanted to be with me? Of course the boy didn't realize we understood what he was saying. He knew we couldn't speak Japanese, but he didn't know we could understand some of it. I know he might feel more comfortable swimming with children like him, but did he have to make his disgust so obvious? Even if we hadn't understood, his facial expressions and tone of voice would have spoken for him. His begging hurt. Did he think that we were so unobservant that he could speak like that in front of us openly?

There are so few internationals in our city that we truly are a novelty item.

Yes, we were foreigners, but that didn't make us completely unaware of people's feelings. I was angry when I left that swimming class. Angry at myself for letting his comment hurt me and angry at the boy for being insensitive. I wanted to show the boy that I was worthy of swimming with him. Making my hurt visible was the last thing I wanted to do.

God, I get so angry at people's comments. There are so few internationals in our city that we truly are a novelty item. We look different, speak differently, and act differently. It seems like they are afraid of us. It seems like they don't want to get to know us. Instead of reaching out to them to make them feel more comfortable, I get angry at them. I make the distance between us even greater. The many insensitive comments soon became a thick wall around my heart to protect myself from the hurtful remarks. As the wall thickened, my anger increased so that any comment would upset me. I want to give my pain and anger to You, God, so You can begin healing me. Please, God, give me grace and courage to reach out to them. Help me see and understand their fear.

Love,
Taylor

WHAT'S HIDDEN IN YOUR HEART?

- Can you think of a time when you haven't understood someone's insensitive comment about you or rude action toward you?

- How can you love someone who hurts you?

- Have you ever built a thick wall around your heart to protect yourself? When and what happened?

- How can understanding the other person's perspective help us respond in a godly way?

- How can God's Word help us when we have negative feelings toward those we are supposed to love?

CHAPTER TEN

I Feel Guilty Because I Don't Like to Go to Church

Dear God, slamming the car door shut, I fastened my seat belt and focused my gaze on the window, trying to direct my thoughts on something other than my steadily increasing fear. I wanted so badly to reverse my actions and head back inside, but my resolve kept me steady. I was going to church. I shouldn't feel this way. I needed to be, truly, the happy pastor's daughter that everyone guessed I was. I shouldn't be fearful and frustrated. And, ultimately, I shouldn't think about myself. I forced myself to stuff my emotions deep down. Summoning my courage and beckoning my resolve, I prayed that those together would lessen my desire to get out of the car, slam the door, and say, "I don't want to go to church."

Going to church was so hard. I didn't understand much, and I never completely knew what I was supposed to do. I honestly just didn't want to go. It was stressful, and I was fearful. The combination of the two always brought on self-pity and misery every Sunday morning while driving to church. Each morning, I would stare out the window and ask You why You were making *me* go through this. Why didn't You take the pain away? Why was everything so hard?

I knew You had placed me in the perfect place to shine, but why didn't I have the courage to do it? I never really acknowledged my guilt, and I never quite understood it. Not going to church wasn't an option, but going with the right attitude was something I was constantly struggling with. I was a missionary kid, but I didn't feel like one. What TCK wouldn't want to go to church? I felt like a candle covered by a basket, like the "love pitcher" completely dried out. *What was wrong with me?* I wanted You to give me what it took to be the person of my expectations, but I always felt lacking.

> *I know not wanting to go to church sounds terrible, almost sinful. But it's the truth.*

As we got out of the car to enter church each Sunday morning, I felt nervous and scared. I didn't understand what I was feeling, and it made me insecure. I wanted so badly to be a good missionary's daughter, to be courageous, but I was fearful and felt so guilty.

I know not wanting to go to church sounds terrible, almost sinful. But it's the truth. It wasn't because I was rebellious. It was because I was so scared of the unknown, so frustrated because things were difficult. I wasn't growing spiritually at church because I didn't understand the teaching. I wasn't even worshipping at church because I didn't understand the songs. I wasn't fellowshipping at church because I couldn't talk to anyone. I was just there because I had to be. So how can church be real to me? I am starting to see that most of my negative emotions stem from being self-focused. I view everything by how it impacts me and makes me feel. My inward focus has placed a negative view on everything.

If only I could see things the way You see them. If only I could see others the way You see them. If only I could see Your desire for my life. God, help me turn my eyes first to You. Please teach me how to take my eyes from myself and turn them to think of others and ways to love them.

Love,
Taylor

WHAT'S HIDDEN IN YOUR HEART?

- What is your church experience like in your country?

- Can you think of a time when you were more focused on yourself than on other people and you began to experience a deluge of negative thoughts and fears?

- How can we understand and embrace God's plan for us when it seems so hard?

- How can God's Word help us change from being self-focused to other-focused?

- How can our relationship with God change our negative attitudes and fears?

PART II
· · · · · · ·

Up to this point, all I could see was the pain in my life. I remembered the hardships but forced myself to believe that everything was okay. Instead of exploring all the negative emotions and dealing with them, I stuffed them deeper in my heart. I was the "pastor's daughter" after all, and it wasn't right for me to feel those things.

How could I feel bitter about the situations I was placed in when God had called me to experience them? How could I be angry at God? It was wrong, I knew, but the questions kept resurfacing. Am I really, truly angry at God? I knew the answer, but I wasn't ready to accept it. I was a missionary kid, and I knew that TCKs shouldn't feel what I was feeling.

When an emotion surfaced, I didn't know what to do with it. Once again, I hid the emotion in my heart. It was so much easier to hide it than to deal with it. As those first few years passed, my heart began to fill with anger, frustration, hopelessness, and bitterness. Something was wrong with me, I realized guiltily. Normal TCKs don't feel this. It was just me.

Until this time of processing in America, I believed that joy and pain were like mountains and valleys. When you were in the valleys, you would be surrounded by pain. Then, after hard work and effort, you would reach the top of the mountain again. You would experience joy for a little while before once again plummeting into the valley. The process would be repeated again and again.

For the first three years in Japan, I felt like I was constantly in a valley. Trying to find my way amidst the fog, I would choose my own paths to deal with the problems. Though I tried to climb the mountain, I always fell. And when my goal was finally in sight, the mountain would grow taller and the paths more confusing and tedious. I felt like I was going in circles. I was afraid to tell my parents because I didn't want them to know what I was really feeling.

I began asking God why He wouldn't intervene when hardships came. I tried so hard to obey Him. Why wasn't He protecting me? Why wasn't He taking the pain away? Why did I feel like I was constantly in the middle of a valley?

It wasn't until I listed all of the negative emotions and wrote all of the prayers about them, that I began to see the positive. I began to see how God had responded, provided, comforted, loved, protected, and guided me through the past four years. I began to see that He actually was there, just in different ways than I expected. He was guiding me; I just wouldn't trust Him with the destination. And though unwilling to take them away, He was willing to comfort me when hardships came.

I began to see so much joy in my life that I had missed. I had been so focused on my personal pain that I had completely missed the blessings in my life. My self-focus had hidden the little gifts of love on the roadside. I had ignored the hand, tenderly reaching down to help me, and I had overlooked the voice in my heart, offering me so much in return for something as small and simple as trust.

As you read the first part of this book, it was probably overwhelming. There was no joy in what I had experienced. No thankfulness in my prayers. No hope in my heart, just constant frustration, bitterness, and anger. For the first four years, that's all I felt. But now that I have allowed the negative emotions to surface and realized my anger at God, He has begun showing me how He blessed my life. I want to show you a glimpse into the blessings. God has tenderly loved me over the past four years.

CHAPTER ELEVEN

. . . .

I Feel Uplifted by One Small Act of Kindness

Dear God, cupping my hands over my mouth and nose, I exhaled slowly, letting my warm breath heat my face. The night before had brought a light snow, and I could see the icy remains of its visit lying in dirty piles beside the road. The street was hidden beneath a blanket of mud and melting snow, and I knew the children at the preschool would be disappointed at the prospect of spending the rest of their afternoon inside. I adjusted my shoe bag onto my other shoulder and untangled my scarf. Smiling, I heard the playful laughter of the children inside the preschool. I opened the heavy gate, slipped inside, and changed shoes. Putting my muddy outdoor shoes in the cabinet at my left, I greeted the principal and hurried to my classroom.

Volunteering at the preschool was something that I never really looked forward to, but my doubts always vanished when ten five-year-olds, all screaming my name, dropped their toys and ran to hug me, comb my blonde hair with Legos, and stand before me, bug-eyed and slack-jawed when I told them I was 13, not 36. The children looked up at me with such expectation and innocence.

This was our last week before spring break, and I had not only grown to know the children, but many had begun to wiggle their way into my heart. I was always wondering what they would grow up to be, or what they went home to every afternoon. Panic always struck when I realized many of those children will never get to know You. Time and time again the realization hit that it was up to me to share Your love. I realized that I might be their only chance to hear of Your gift of love in this life and eternally in the next.

I was thinking about these things as I left that last afternoon. I was saying goodbye and thanking the teachers when one of my favorite little girls came up shyly. When I turned around and smiled at her, she lost a bit of timidity and handed me a letter. She grinned proudly as she told me that she had drawn it by herself, and she wanted to give it to my sister and me. I took the letter and thanked her. She giggled.

> *I realized that I might be their only chance to hear of Your gift of love in this life and eternally in the next.*

Her sweet little face turned upward as she took my hand, squeezed it gently, and told me goodbye before skipping back into the classroom. What had I done to deserve their special attention and gifts? I hadn't a clue. But it made me feel special and wanted. I felt certain this was the way that You loved, pure and unashamedly. Freely and willingly. *But could I love like this?* I didn't know. The children at the preschool had taught me a way of loving that I hadn't really seen before, a way that I longed to possess.

Later at home, I opened the letter. She had drawn a picture of herself, Sydney and me holding hands. She had also written a note thanking us and telling us that she would miss us. I was so blessed by that little note, so uplifted by her thoughtfulness and sweetness. I now see the gift that You had so gently placed in my hands, and I am amazed at Your thoughtfulness in yet another situation. You were seeking to make us feel more secure and more excited about going back. You reassured me that though the things You had placed in my life were small, they would add up to something bigger. I thanked the little girl that day and treasured that note all summer long. I want to thank You for Your thoughtfulness that day. I want to thank You for Your reassurance: the little things I was doing had begun to add up, directed toward a bigger and greater purpose.

Love,
Taylor

WHAT'S HIDDEN IN YOUR HEART?

- As a TCK, think of a time when you were touched by the gift or action of a national.

- Make a list of all the people in your life that God has used to encourage you. How has He used each one?

- Think of a time when you did something extremely simple for someone else, but God used it in a huge way.

- What does God's Word say about doing the "little things"?

CHAPTER TWELVE

I Feel Amazed By the Courage of the Japanese Christians

Dear God, "Before you leave our home, we have a surprise that we have prepared for you." I looked up into the beaming face of O—san. This sweet couple had spent so much money and time on us already, and I wondered what else they could possibly give us. Clearing his throat, O—san grinned once more. "I want to sing for you a special hymn tonight. It's my favorite." He ducked his head as we clapped; he was clearly embarrassed at the attention he was receiving.

"I will sing the first verse in Japanese, and I will try my hardest to sing the second verse in English. I hope you approve. My English is not so good."

After moving to Japan, I realized quickly the Japanese people rarely invited others to their homes. Eating dinner together as a family was usually impossible because of the father's work schedule. Though our house was always open, I really wanted to go to a Japanese family's house for dinner. I had only been in a few Japanese homes since we moved to Japan, and most of them were very formal. But the first invitation for dinner was one that I will never forget.

One of our favorite older couples from church asked us to

their home for dinner. We accepted the invitation but were unprepared for what would happen after dinner. Like most Japanese people do when guests visit their home, they bought the most expensive meats and vegetables and prepared a huge meal for us. They cleaned their house thoroughly and directed us to the nicest seats and dishes during dinner. I was amazed at their humility and eagerness to understand us better, but when the older couple told us they had prepared something special for us after dinner, I was overwhelmed. Heart flipping, I watched as he nodded for his wife to begin playing the piano. His hands shook as he held the song book, but I could see the joy he possessed as he sang to You.

Who would have thought that our family would be able to worship with believers who spoke a different language and lived in a different culture.

As I thought back over that time together, I realized that I had experienced something special. Who would have thought that our family would be able to worship together with believers who spoke a different language and lived in a different culture... all the way across the world? They gave us a gift that no other Japanese person has ever given. They gave us a glimpse into their hearts. They obeyed Your wish in letting You tear down a little bit of the wall of culture surrounding them, and they allowed their love for You to flow from them to us.

I was overwhelmed at their humility, God, and their willingness in allowing You to work through them and in them. Right then, I wanted to have that same crazy, child-like love for You that I saw on the O—sans face. They had made the decision to be loved and to love like You no matter the cost. They had taken a risk to invite us over in spite of the language barrier, and I knew they had left their comfort zones to minister to us.

I realize now how much You desire me to do the same: to give the Japanese people a glimpse into my heart and to allow You to tear down my wall of fear. You have asked me to surrender myself to You, surrounding me with Your love, so in return, I could love the Japanese with that same passion and intensity.

I saw in them a courage that I lack. God, help me to push beyond my fear in order to share Your love to the Japanese. I saw a glimpse of Your love radiating from the O—sans that night, and I want to have that same joy that I saw so unashamedly on their faces. I want to surrender so that I can love like You... no matter the cost.

Love,
Taylor

WHAT'S HIDDEN IN YOUR HEART?

- Think about the national Christians in your city. How do they show courage in their daily walk with Christ?

- What have you learned from watching the national Christians?

- How has your fear prevented you or slowed you in showering love on the nationals in your city?

- What does God say about our fears? How can He help us?

CHAPTER THIRTEEN

I Feel Loved by the Growing Relationships With Others

Dear God, taking a deep breath, I willed my fingers to stop shaking as I adjusted my music sheet on the baby grand piano before me. The piano was dusted and its keys were sparkling. I knew the precious older couple waiting eagerly beside me had spent the majority of their afternoon preparing the piano for me.

About three years after moving to Japan, we received a handwritten invitation from an older couple at church inviting us to share dinner with them in their home. In the invitation, they had asked me to bring my piano music so that I could play for them. I was nervous about going for the first time but was excited that yet another sweet older couple from church had invited us to their home for a meal.

As soon as I walked into the front door I realized how much time they had spent preparing for our night together. The house was spotless, and their adult daughter had spent the night with them, cooking most of the dinner so the elderly wife could handle the pressure of company. They had planned the whole evening, timing and everything, on paper and followed the list strictly throughout the whole evening. The husband had even written an English prayer beforehand so he would be ready to pray before we ate. I was overwhelmed at their preparation for this night, and I realized how much courage it took for a couple so traditional to invite us into their home.

After I finished playing my piano piece, Mrs. T sat my sister and me down at the coffee table next to the piano. My heart flipped when I saw the twinkle in her eye as she told us to make ourselves at home. "I'm going to prepare a special surprise for you," she said. "Now wait here... I'll be right back."

A few minutes later, she came back, carrying a tray filled with tall glasses of expensive rice wine and traditional cakes filled with white and red beans. She made sure we ate our fill before pulling out two bags from under her seat. She beamed as she handed the first bag to my sister and the second bag to me. "These are just a few small gifts I wanted to give you for accepting our invitation for dinner." As we thanked her and asked her if we were allowed to open it, she nodded her head quickly. "Of course you may. I hope you like it." She giggled shyly as we opened our gifts, embarrassed when we offered our thanks. "No... thank you. We are so honored to have your family to our home for dinner." As I stared at my new music scores and Sydney looked at her art supplies, I felt so loved.

After a few moments of silence, she nodded to herself as if in confirmation, and then she began speaking in the sweetest of tones. She asked us if we would allow her and her husband to be our Japanese grandparents. She told us that she realized how hard it must have been to leave our American grandparents, and they wanted to help us transition into our new country.

That made me feel so special, so cherished. What had I done to deserve such a special place in their hearts? I was dumbfounded. Ever since that first Sunday in Japan, they had always been sure to speak to me after church, and the husband made sure to speak to me in English. And his wife always smiled. I was amazed at their generosity and eagerness to be a part in my life. They had immediately realized that living in another country was always accompanied with losses, and they were trying their hardest to show me how much they cared.

You had placed us in their heart, but it took me so long to see that their kindness was actually a gift from You. I loved the way Mr. T phrased his English and how Mrs. T wanted so desperately to love us like her own. Their open love for us magnified their steady love for You, and I saw how such a traditional couple had broken tradition in order to obey

> *You had placed us in their heart, but it took me so long to see that their kindness was actually a gift from You.*

Your calling. You had called them to love, and they had gone beyond my highest expectations.

I now see so clearly how much You were trying to love me. I felt alone with no friends or relationships. You were opening doors to people's hearts, and wanting me to trust You. For the first three years, I couldn't understand why Mr. T talked to me each Sunday. I didn't think it was all that important. I didn't expect Your love to come from older people at church. I wanted young friends, so I was blind to Your provisions. You knew what I needed, but I had gripped the lock and hidden the key to the door of my heart, not trusting that You were strong enough to be in control.

I now see that you were providing people to love me. You were surrounding me with older couples who wanted to love me, even with all my differences and lack of language. When

I opened my eyes to see Your goodness, I was so surprised. I just didn't see.

Love,
Taylor

WHAT'S HIDDEN IN YOUR HEART?

- Think of some unexpected friendships in your life. How did these relationships surprise you?

- Can you think of a time when God was working all around you for your own good, but you didn't see it? When did you see it, and what happened?

- Examine your life right now. Are there areas where you feel that God has forsaken you? How might He be working for your good?

- How can we be encouraged by Jeremiah 29:11?

CHAPTER FOURTEEN

. . . .

I Feel Encouraged by the Relationships God Is Opening

Dear God, my heart skipped at the twinkle in my Kumon teacher's eye as she motioned for me to come to her desk. Seeing the pad of paper on the table in front of her, I grinned and said, "You write a question first, and I'll answer." I was attending a Japanese after-school study program, where I was learning Japanese for foreigners. This was the first time my teacher had ever taught the program, and she wasn't sure how to help me.

Laughing she flipped the paper around, grabbed a pencil, and began writing my first question in Japanese. I pulled up a stool, waiting for the question she would give me. I tried to think of an answer I might give back in Japanese.

Months earlier, I would finish my homework early. Since my sister sometimes took longer than I did, I would sit at my desk, self-conscious and embarrassed because of my Japanese work sitting on the desk in front of me. Though the children tried hard not to be conspicuous, I saw them lean over, look at my work, and grin at its childish Japanese. I knew I was being ridiculous, but it was so embarrassing when eight-year-olds giggled at my Japanese, and then they began reciting parts in the stories where I struggled the most.

It was then when I quickly began to make friends with our Kumon teacher. She was fascinated with American culture, and she wanted to understand our lives better. My sensei knew I felt self-conscious about my work, and she didn't want time wasted in learning more about us.

The next week, she brought a notebook with her. Since I could write in Japanese better than I could speak it, we began writing to each other. If she didn't understand what I was trying to write, I would try to explain it in Japanese as best I could, and eventually, she would understand what I was trying to say.

I had yet to make any true friends at the playground, and I felt more confident speaking with adults because I knew they wouldn't laugh at me.

Our friendship grew much stronger during that time at Kumon. She learned lots about our lives and American culture, and in turn, she began to reveal the secrets of her own culture. I was fascinated with the culture that surrounded me, and when I had questions, I would write them down and ask her each Tuesday. My understanding of the culture grew rapidly. I was so encouraged through that time with her.

I had yet to make any true friends at the playground, and I felt more confident speaking with adults because I knew they wouldn't laugh at me. I realize now that this experience was probably the first time that I truly saw You working. At Kumon, it helped me ignore the stares and focus on the friendship unfolding before me, and I could see You slowly softening my teacher's heart as I shared about Christianity.

Though my teacher was reserved about coming to our home for Christmas parties each December, I could tell she was curious about why we had moved to Japan. After going to Kumon for two years, I had the opportunity to give my teacher a Bible. She had said that she would be interested in reading about Christianity. So we bought a bilingual Bible, and I gave it to her as a gift. Our relationship continued to deepen.

With each class, You were encouraging me to come out of my shell a bit more and to open my eyes to see how You were working. I want to continue to open my eyes, God, and to see Your hand working in Japan. You were placing key people in my life to encourage me and to help me grow in cultural understanding and language acquisition.

Love,
Taylor

WHAT'S HIDDEN IN YOUR HEART?

- Who are the key people that God has places in your life to teach you culture and language?

- How have these people encouraged you?

- In what ways have you been able to share God's love with these people?

- What is your process of developing a growing relationship with someone who is from a different culture?

CHAPTER FIFTEEN

I Feel Thankful for God's Provision of a Christian Japanese
Language Teacher

Dear God, when we quit Kumon (a Japanese study school) to pursue a different language study focused on listening and speaking, I was fearful. My teacher was the only friend that I felt completely comfortable speaking Japanese with, and I didn't think You would provide another language teacher like her. I didn't realize You had better plans, and I couldn't trust in Your timing for them.

Months passed, and we still didn't have a new teacher. I was starting to worry that I would forget my Japanese. Going to church was the hardest at that point, and I was fearful that stopping language studies would make it even harder. But I still refused to trust You, shouldering my worry with the resolution of solving the problem by myself.

That fall, we decided to visit some missionaries in Yamaguchi ken, about four hours from our house in Hiroshima. As we talked with the other missionaries, we mentioned that we were looking for a new language teacher. They told us about their former teacher, who was a Christian. She had taught them the religious vocabulary that they had needed in order to start speaking without translation in their churches. I listened intently. I didn't need religious vocabulary in order to speak, but it would be so much easier to understand the Japanese sermons if I had a foundation.

We met their language teacher the next day, and we agreed that it would be best for her to come to our city and, in addition, to teach lessons via Skype. Every Wednesday, we would pay for her train ticket to Hiroshima. She would teach us lessons in between meals and spend the night, then leave the following morning.

I began understanding so much of what I heard. The only thing stopping me from speaking was my fear.

"Please write a prayer for me in English. Then I will translate it into Japanese. I want you to memorize it and pray before each class," our new teacher said. Our eyes widened. How could we do that? She went on teaching Kanji, and then she started telling us a story.

"If you don't know a word, stop me," she said as she began talking very quickly. Soon our hands were up, expecting an explanation in English. She explained the meaning a different way in Japanese and drew pictures to help. That first story included charades, pictures, and pauses, but we understood it all—all in Japanese.

At the end of the lesson, she said, "Here is your homework. I expect that you pray in Japanese each day and learn all of your new vocabulary. Also, look up all of these verses in Japanese."

My Japanese began to improve very quickly. She refused to

speak to us in English, even though she had the ability. Her main concern was our language, not hers.

I was so thankful for our new language teacher, God. It gave me so much hope that church would get easier. Since we studied religious vocabulary, reading verses in Japanese got so much easier, and we were beginning to understand parts of the sermon at church. Suddenly, I began understanding so much of what I heard. But the only thing stopping me from speaking was my fear.

I thanked her many times for coming to teach us, but as I look back, I realize I had never thanked You. I now see what was missing, God. I see my ungrateful spirit. I want to thank You now, even if it's a year late, for how much You did for me. You were the One, after all, who provided our new language teacher. You were the One asking me to trust You to provide what we needed, when we needed it. You were there all along! But I was ignoring everything. I wasn't seeking You, and I was trying to carry the burden all by myself.

In the midst of my language studies and at the height of my hopelessness, You gave me hope. You provided for me.

Love,
Taylor

WHAT'S HIDDEN IN YOUR HEART?

- Think of a time when you tried to solve your problems without God.
- Why is it so hard to trust that God will provide what we need, when we need it?
- How would you define "hope in God"?

CHAPTER SIXTEEN

I Feel Like I Belong When I'm Serving

Dear God, running down the aisle to the back of the church, I smiled when the children beside me stared in amazement at my Egyptian costume. I had just finished a skit at our first Vacation Bible School in Japan, and I needed to get down to the English classroom before the kids came. I untied the paper belt, slid the toga off, and placed my paper head covering on top. I grinned, laughing when some of the children gawked at my regular clothes underneath, confusion framing their faces. Hurrying down the steps to the English room, I began helping prepare for the first round of children. This was so much fun!

As I laid out the English crafts on the table and wrote English names on the white board, I listened to children's laughter at the Bible story skit upstairs. It was so amazing to be able to experience this. I felt Your presence at church. I felt like You were with me, and I was so content.

I see now how You were working, God. I was so focused on myself, so focused on hiding my negative emotions from other people that I rarely noticed how You were working. You were showing me how much joy can come out of serving others and serving You. We had been having Kids' English Club for over a year. But each Saturday that we went, I didn't really want to serve because I was afraid the kids wouldn't like me or I wouldn't know what to do. I was afraid I might have to say something, and the kids would laugh at my accent.

For four years, we have been doing special children's outreaches. But again, I held back, not wanting to truly engage in service. I didn't mind the preparation work at home because that was safe. But I didn't engage in service because I was more concerned about protecting me than ministering to them.

I see now how You were working, God. I was so focused on myself, that I rarely noticed how You were working.

When the team from our home church came to Japan to serve at VBS, they did so much. I joined them in service, and You taught me so much. You showed me that I can only experience true joy and contentment when I focus on serving others and stop focusing on protecting myself from embarrassment. I fell in love with the same kids that I previously had not wanted to connect with. I couldn't believe how you were changing my heart and challenging me to overcome my fears.

As the doors opened and children filed through the double doors in front of me, I wondered how I could have missed this. I see how You were working all along, and I want to focus my attention on You instead of me.

Love,
Taylor

WHAT'S HIDDEN IN YOUR HEART?

- How do you serve the Lord in your country?

- Think about a time when you didn't want to engage in service because of your fear.

- What has God taught you through serving Him?

- Explain a time when you were so blessed because of your service to God.

CHAPTER SEVENTEEN

. . . .

I Feel Thankful Because Other Japanese Friends Left Their Comfort Zone In Order to Connect with Me

Dear God, smiling, I wove through a crowd of people at the mall and waited for my friends to join me in line at Starbucks. This was one of our usual stops when we were together, and I was looking forward to a cold drink. I saw some of the regular Starbucks workers behind the counter. After ordering my drink, I hurried over to the second counter, catching a grin from one of my favorite girls who worked there. We talked for a few minutes before she handed me my drink. I detected an abnormal sparkle in her eye, but chose to ignore it. Her smile was adorable, and she wasn't the type to keep secrets.

When we first moved to Japan we went to the mall every week, and Starbucks was always one of our weekly stops. In the beginning, we would order by pointing to a coffee on the menu and holding up two fingers, but as our language increased, we began to talk with the girls working at Starbucks more and more. Our favorite girl, who usually took our order, would always come over and talk to us even after we got our drinks. Her beautiful, inviting smile was something I looked forward to each week. After a few months, other employees wanted to talk to us. Soon, we knew several employees all by name.

Looking around, I hurried and sat down at a table before taking a sip of my drink. I looked down at the table when something caught my eye. My smile widened when I saw the "good morning" that she had written in English on my cup. Catching her eye, I nodded my head in thanks, heart flipping when I saw her grin back at me.

> *I wanted to love others, but I was unwilling to lay down my pride.*

Three years earlier, the kids on the playground had laughed at me because of my poor Japanese. That was when I had made the promise to myself to not speak Japanese until I understood the language perfectly and could respond in perfect Japanese. I was determined not to go out of my comfort zone. From that point on, I remained silent. I refused to speak even if I could. Then my silence became a habit, a way of life. My silence soon became my prison, for I didn't know how to break out and begin speaking.

Even for the sake of others, I continued to refuse to break my silence, and yet I watched this Starbucks worker go completely out of her comfort zone. Why? To make *me* feel more comfortable. I saw the beautiful "Good morning!" written on my cup, and I was so humbled.

I felt You tug at my heart as I sat down with my friends. It was like You were saying, "See how much I love you? Now I want you to lay down your pride and love others. Going out of your comfort zone is something I am asking you to do." I wanted to love others, but I was unwilling to lay down my pride. I didn't know how to change.

Going out of my comfort zone seemed too risky. You were calling me to surrender to Your will, and I refused. And I kept refusing—the entire time we were in Japan. But now I have another opportunity to come out of my comfort zone when we return to Japan. I don't want to love from a distance, but to love like You love, openly and extravagantly. I want to take advantage of this opportunity, God, and to love like someone on fire for You.

Love,
Taylor

WHAT'S HIDDEN IN YOUR HEART?

· Explain a time when you left your comfort zone to love someone.

· What exactly is a "comfort zone"? Why do we have them?

· How can a "comfort zone" be a good thing? How can it be a bad thing?

· What does it feel like to be "in the zone" and to be "out of the zone"?

CHAPTER EIGHTEEN

. . . .

I Feel Humbled When Another Child Protected Me

Dear God, keeping my tears in check, I bowed my head, telling myself to ignore the teasing coming in my direction. The boys didn't mean it, I knew, and they didn't even know I understood it, but it still hurt. I did my best to wipe the hurt off my face. We were in the middle of Sunday school, and I needed to focus on what the teacher was saying or I wouldn't understand what we were doing next.

In a way, going to the chapel was the easiest and hardest thing to do. Some of the children wanted to be our friend, and like the boys teasing me, others didn't. I never quite knew what to expect when I went to church. But the teachers were kind, and they were always trying their hardest to make me feel accepted.

Doing my best not to let the hurt and embarrassment show on my face, I listened to the teacher beside me. I had told myself to forget the comments and turn back toward the teacher when a sweet little girl sitting across from me stuck her hand up in the air, eyes glued to mine. *Uh oh...* I focused my gaze somewhere else, scrunching my shoulders. What was happening now? By the way she looked at me, I knew she had seen my unsuccessful attempts at ignorance. She had seen the hurt on my face when the boys teased me, and the determined look on her face told me she wanted to do something about it.

Standing up, she raised her hand and shouted for everyone to be quiet. Then she said, "I just want to remind everyone to be kind to the foreigners." Looking directly at the boys sitting next to her, she continued after a purposeful pause. "We need to speak slowly in Japanese, too. That way they can understand what we are saying."

> *If I didn't have the courage to stand up for someone's feelings, would I have courage to stand up for my beliefs?*

From past experiences, I knew this girl wouldn't tolerate any misbehavior after her requests, and I could see a desire for our friendship rising to the surface of her heart. I was ready to take it, but I wasn't sure how.

What had urged this girl, during the Sunday school lesson, to stand up for two foreigners who hadn't a clue what was happening ninety percent of the time? Did this nine-year-old girl really want to be friends with us? Questions rushed to my mind as I watched her take her seat. After a moment the little girl looked up, and a beautiful grin lit her face when she saw me smiling at her.

I was completely humbled.

I seriously doubted if I would have the courage to stand up for someone who had never talked to me before. In fact, I knew that I wouldn't have. This nine-year-old girl had more courage than I did. That grin made me feel special and wanted, but afterward the realization hit. If I didn't have the courage to stand up for someone's feelings, would I have the courage to stand up for my beliefs? Let alone share it with others?

It was then that I started asking You why You had called *me* to Japan. You obviously saw my lack of courage and conviction. Why did You choose someone so shy? Why not choose someone like the girl who had stood up for me? She had the courage to do everything.

Why? Why? Why? I have asked You that question year after year after year. Why did You choose me, God? Why not someone else, better fit to fulfill Your purposes? But God, I realize... You had chosen our family, including *me*. Not because of our strength, not because of our courage, not because of our conviction, not because of our humility, but because we said "yes," yes to Your calling and yes to Your will.

In all actuality, I didn't say "yes." I went to Japan because my parents said we were going. I didn't know what to expect, so I had no fears. When I realized how hard the language was and how difficult it is to understand the culture, I began saying, "No, I don't really want to do this." My parents' call is not my call. The past four years, You have been showing me that Japan is Your special call for my life, too. You want me to surrender, to submit to Your perfect plan for my life. You want me to stand up for those who do not know You.

When that young girl stood up to protect me, I was humbled by her courage. She defended the weak. Father, You are asking me to stand up, to step out of my fear and share Your love. It is so easy for me to see all of life revolving around me and my needs. Please teach me to see life as You see it and to be willing to love others as You do.

Love,
Taylor

WHAT'S HIDDEN IN YOUR HEART?

· ·

- Can you think of a time when someone protected you?

- What is the difference between God's mission call for your parents and God's call for your life?

- Think of a time when you were angry or bitter that God had called your parents into missions.

- Describe the difference between seeing the big picture for your life and living the small picture for your life.

CHAPTER NINETEEN

. . . .

I Feel Courageous When I Take a Risk to Connect

Dear God, *nervous...* it hardly began to describe the emotions tumbling through my brain as I locked the front door and started down the dimly lit street before me. Linking arms with my friend, I buttoned up my winter coat before turning the corner.

My heart had lurched when I saw the bus stop at the bottom of the mountain. *God... I need You...* Courage faltering, I clenched my fists. This was going to be a good sleepover if I could muster up the courage to make it happen. But what if I didn't have it? What would happen then? I shook my fears and shoved my unanswered questions away for the hundredth time. Telling myself that my fear was ridiculous, I prayed for resolve. *I'm surrendering, Jesus. My fear is holding me captive. I'm asking for courage, I don't have enough on my own.*

We had already invited all of the girls from church to a sleepover at our house once before, and though awkward, it had been fun. The major obstacle in getting to know them better was language, and that frustrated me. This time around, only one girl from youth group and her friend came.

We also invited our Japanese-Korean friends who speak

both Japanese and English well. They were planning to help with language. We knew that they would be able to connect with the girls better than we could, and we wanted them to feel comfortable. Our friends came to our house early, and we prepared for the sleepover together. I was really nervous about a second sleepover, but I was also excited. I was hoping we would connect with the two other girls.

We met the other girls at 8:00 in the evening and walked them up from the bus stop to our home. After we ate dinner together, we played simple English word games. Japanese girls aren't allowed to have their nails painted on weekdays,

The more deeply I know You, the easier it will be to trust You.

and they were excited when my sister, Sydney, painted their nails hot pink. I was thankful for that time to-gether, God, and I really felt like You were there giving me courage to step out of my comfort zone. It was like You were saying. "See? If you step out in faith and obey Me, I will give You what it takes and more to fulfill My plan and purposes. Trust Me, Taylor, see how I provide?" I saw it then, God. I saw how You provided and filled me with courage.

As I look back over the past four years, I see how You were asking me the same questions. "Trust me. See how I will pro-vide? See how I will give you strength?" But, looking back, I see how my decisions were made based on fear. I was unwilling to take a risk, to step out into the unknown and trust that You would catch me and guide me. After the sleepover, I realized once again the importance of trust. The only way You could give me courage is if I placed myself in a position to need it.

During that sleepover, I saw how You provided, comforted, loved, and guided. I saw how You gave me what it took—how

You gripped my hand as I gripped Yours. Over the past four years, I've seen my mistakes. I haven't trusted You, and that impacted everything. But I want to trust You now. I see how much more fulfilled and satisfied I am when I allow You to give me *Your* strength. I want to give You my heart and trust You, but my fears constantly hold me back. I realize that the more deeply I know You, the easier it will be to trust You.

Love,
Taylor

WHAT'S HIDDEN IN YOUR HEART?

- Think of a time when you took a huge risk and experienced God's strength and guidance.

- Why is it so hard for us to trust God with the details of our lives?

- How does knowing God intimately help us to trust Him more deeply?

- How can Proverbs 3:5&6 give us courage?

CHAPTER TWENTY

I Feel Content When I Let My Walls Down

Dear God, waving goodbye, I grinned at the pastor's daughter before closing the door and adjusting the bag slung across my shoulder. She was so sweet to try to connect with us even though she was in her early twenties. I was sad that our time with the pastor's daughter had ended. Slamming the car door shut, I buckled my seat belt and looked through the frost covered window. Smiling when she waved at me from inside the house, I laughed and waved back.

We had been studying how to read and write Japanese using textbooks, and I really wanted to practice my language by talking with someone. We decided to ask the pastor's daughter. The next Sunday, we asked her about our idea, and she agreed. Like most Japanese girls, she wanted to know more about us but didn't know how to ask. I was a bit nervous about meeting with her for the first time, but I was excited about the opportunity to get to know her better.

Every Thursday evening after eating dinner at her house, we would go into the tatami room with a snack, coffee, three electronic dictionaries, pens, and lots of paper. Then we would talk. We would talk about youth group and You. We would talk about boys and plan our weddings. We would talk about other countries and traveling. I was amazed at how comfortable I felt. How content I felt when I let my walls of fear down... and was just me.

Going to the Japanese pastor's home each week was something I anticipated. It was the only time when I could let my barrier down. After a while, I began asking myself why my wall was up all of the time. Why I was continually hiding behind my wall of fear and shyness? I began to see how blatant my lack of courage was and how fearful I was of the unknown. I think those evenings with the pastor's daughter was Your way of showing me my fear and asking me to step forward in courage.

> *You were trying to show me how wonderful it could be if I stepped out from behind the wall in every relationship.*

It was then that I realized that each time I was fearful, I added another brick to my wall. The problem was that my wall was getting so high and thick that I could not connect with anyone unless it was on my terms—English. When the pastor's daughter spent all of this time with us and I saw that I could connect even with the language barrier, I dropped the wall when I was with her. You were trying to show me how wonderful it could be if I stepped out from behind the wall in every relationship. But I was too afraid.

God, thank you for showing me that You are there and always willing to help me. You tenderly continue to teach, to show me that my walled comfort zone is not Your will for my life.

Love,
Taylor

WHAT'S HIDDEN IN YOUR HEART?

- Do you have a wall of fear blocking certain people from having a relationship with you? How did you build it?

- What happens to a person who never allows God to "tear down the walls"?

- How can fear force us to live in our comfort zones?

- What lesson is God teaching you right now? How does He keep reinforcing the lesson?

CHAPTER TWENTY-ONE

. . . .

I Feel Blessed—Not Lucky

Dear God, fighting the urge to roll my eyes, I bowed my head. I *hated* being called lucky. This was not a life filled with luck—it was so hard. My frustration built as I glanced at our guest across the table.

"Yes, you girls are so very lucky," she repeated. Playing with my chopsticks, I peeked another glance at our guest, anger kindling at her gaze. I tried my best to see things through her eyes, but the image blurred as my questions grew. Did people not see how *hard* it was to live in another country? To be separated from extended family? To not understand the language spoken around you? Yes, God was doing amazing things in Japan, but couldn't people see my view as well?

It wasn't uncommon for us to have American people to our house for dinner. Many times, they would visit one of the Japanese churches. We would get to know them a bit at church and then invite them over for dinner. One evening, we had invited a young couple to our house. We were eating dessert while they asked us about our lives in Japan. I could see them grow wistful as we spoke about the opportunities You were opening, and when we finished, they told my sister and I how lucky we were to have an experience like this.

Lucky. *Lucky.* The word itself had made me question its meaning time and time again.

I excused myself and hurried to my room as our guests continued talking with my parents. My question bubbled close to the surface as I sat at my piano, stretching my fingers and running my hands over its white keys. Did people not understand our lives? It seemed as though when they saw God working in the lives of others, they assumed that He was taking away the hardships and pain in our lives as well. They assumed that everything was just fine and dandy, and that our hearts were fully devoted to the Father. I was fearful to mention otherwise... fearful of their response. I groaned in frustration. *Why did everyone seem to sugarcoat my life?*

Did people not see how hard it was to live in another country?

They looked so longingly at what I had experienced, not realizing what it took to live the way we did. Did no one understand what I was feeling? Or better yet, was it wrong to feel the way I did? I felt stuck. God had done so much for me...but no matter how many words I thought of, I couldn't find a word that described what I truly felt. Lucky meant no hardships, so that wasn't the word I was looking for.

A few days later, we went to another missionary's house for lunch. We had been talking for a while, and they too wanted to know how You were working in our lives. A few moments later, the older couple told my sister and me how blessed we were to have such an experience like this. How blessed we were to see up-close how You are working. To be on the battleground...and see You winning.

Lucky, I felt, was just like chance. Like a toss of the dice or a spin of the wheel. But blessings, I felt, were like love gifts from You, beautiful experiences we ought to cherish, ones that were planned and intended just for us. I want to see the blessings amidst the hardships, God. I want to see the joy amidst the pain. I know I can't do it on my own, but I want You to open my eyes so I can see Your light shining through the hardships of life. Yes, I am blessed, not lucky.

Love,
Taylor

WHAT'S HIDDEN IN YOUR HEART?

- Have you ever been told how lucky you are to be the son or daughter of a missionary?
- List all of the things that feel a little "unlucky" about your life overseas.
- Compare the meaning of "lucky" and "blessed."
- List all of the ways that you truly are blessed by God through the experiences of being a TCK.

CHAPTER TWENTY-TWO

· ·

Conclusion

Being a TCK is hard. Moving to another culture in the name of Jesus is always accompanied by the powerful hand of Satan. His darkness is strong, and it's incredibly difficult, sometimes, to resist his always so tempting deceit. Unknowingly, I had begun to allow Satan's fingertips to enclose my heart, realizing his greed for strongholds in his own battle, but unaware that he was relying on my own weakness to build them.

I had been so oblivious to God's true desires when I moved to Japan. I built myself up with the knowledge of my obedience, thinking myself already committed to God in every way. With my pride at my side, I had stepped forward into the unknown, sure that God had already taught me the lessons He was trying to teach me, and that I, in turn, was fully pliable to be used for His glory. All at the age of nine!

I was ignorant to the fact that the most important, most daunting, most stretching, and most difficult lessons were to be taught *on* the field, not *before* it. Yes, God was using this experience to shine His light in a country immersed in darkness, but that was not His only reason. God was using this experience to shine His light in the darkness of my own heart—to reveal my weaknesses and to highlight the strongholds of pride, selfishness, fear, and anger. Like layers of an onion, God was tenderly pulling away each tough layer to reach His ultimate goal, a soft and workable heart, devoted to serving Him.

As God began peeling away my tough layers of worldly desires, He also began putting worldly circumstances in my path, not to harm me, but to stretch me. It was my choice how to deal with them, and I chose poorly. I chose to believe Satan's lies. And I chose to believe that God was against me, not for me.

During this home assignment in America, I truly felt like I was at my end. God had asked me to reach a little higher than my body would allow, and stretch a little farther than my ability. I was angry at God for not giving me fewer hardships, frustrated at His lack of concern, and bitter because of His expectations. Though it seems strange and almost cruel at times, in the end, His desire *was* my brokenness. The place where I ended was the starting line for where He began. If I had trusted in Him, He would have given me the "more" I needed to accomplish His will.

I feel almost like I had explored every option other than trust. I had tried every other path than His. I had never truly *listened* to His voice. And though I yearned for it, I had taken every other means of guidance and protection than His. I had depended upon my own strength, and it had given out. I had followed my own path, and I had gotten lost. I'd even attempted to rely on my own wisdom, and it had led me in the wrong direction. I had avoided Jesus because of how hard it was to put my complete and utter trust in Him. But He's given me another chance to re-examine the past four years, to discover the true contents hidden in my heart.

Each one of us has a life story, don't we? We all relive stories hidden in our heart, some coupled with emotions that we don't quite understand. All of us question God's goodness at some point in our lives and cry out to Him in anger and fear when we can't feel His presence. Each one of us experiences shame and sorrow, and we allow strongholds in our hearts that we just can't quite give to Jesus yet. Everyone has experienced anger and bitterness, contentment and encouragement.

He's given me another chance to re-examine the past four years, to discover the true contents hidden in my heart.

Your prayers just might have a different twist than mine, and your questions to the Father might still be unanswered. But I'm learning, through both the joys and hardships, through both my anger at Him and His forgiveness toward me, that no matter what walls I have, and no matter how ignorant I am of His love, that He's always ready to love and treasure me, whether I choose paths for His glory or for mine. I didn't know all these things were hidden in my heart. I didn't even realize that I was angry at God.

I have finished my prayers. God has let me "relive" the past four years, teaching me and showing me His presence. We will return to Japan soon. Am I ready? Have I learned anything? Will I be consumed with fear? Will I get angry at God again? I don't know. But I am praying that I will trust Him. I am praying that I will cling to Him and see how blessed I really am.

Connect with Taylor and other TCKs at
Facebook.com/HiddeninMyHeartBook